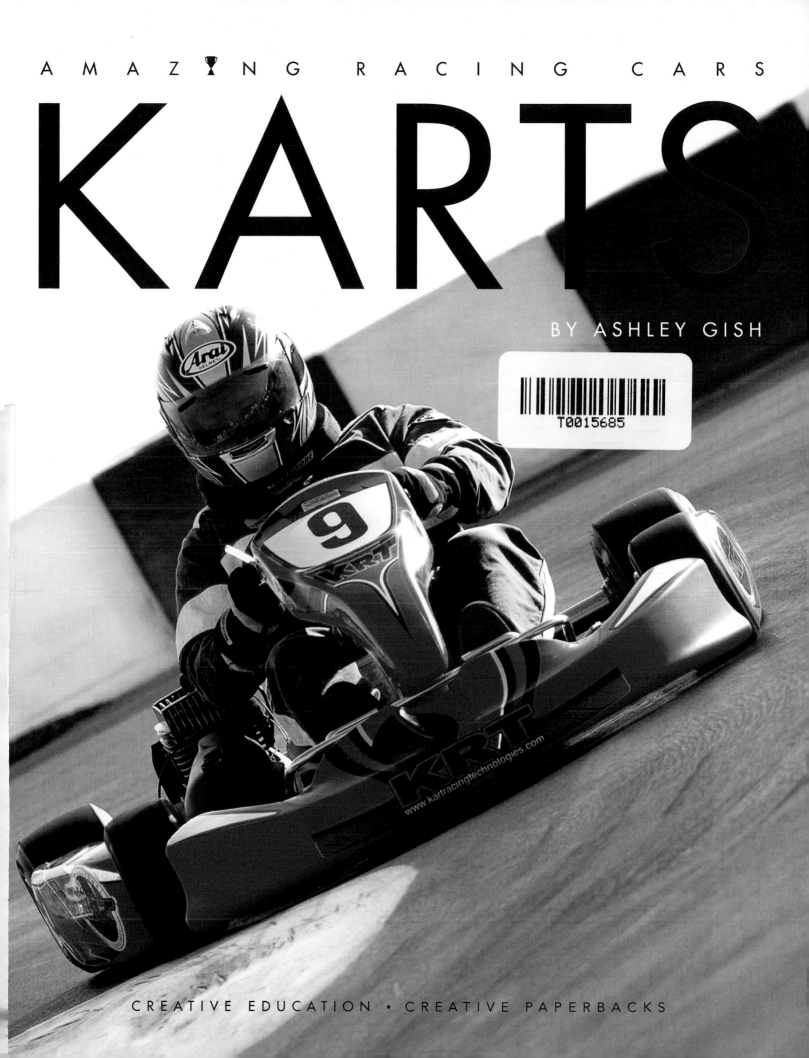

AMAZING RACING CARS
KARTS

BY ASHLEY GISH

CREATIVE EDUCATION • CREATIVE PAPERBACKS

Published by Creative Education and Creative Paperbacks
P.O. Box 227, Mankato, Minnesota 56002
Creative Education and Creative Paperbacks are imprints of
The Creative Company
www.thecreativecompany.us

Design by The Design Lab
Production by Joe Kahnke
Art direction by Rita Marshall
Printed in China

Photographs by Alamy (imageBROKER, Loolee, mauritius images
GMBH, MAURO DALLA POZZA, Travis VanDenBerg), Dreamstime
(Clickandphoto), Getty Images (Pat Brollier/The Enthusiast Network),
Pinal Central (Oscar Perez), Shutterstock (Steve Mann, Roland Mag-
nusson, Terry Poche, Vdant85), SuperStock (look photos)

Image on p. 13 courtesy of Scott Wilson.

Library of Congress Cataloging-in-Publication Data
Names: Gish, Ashley, author.
Title: Karts / Ashley Gish.
Series: Amazing racing cars.
Includes bibliographical references and index.
Summary: A fast-paced, high-interest introduction to karts, open-
wheeled racing vehicles known for their strong chassis and use in
a variety of races. Also included is a biographical story about kart
driver Mia Chapman.
Identifiers: LCCN: 2019049509
ISBN 978-1-64026-288-1 (hardcover)
ISBN 978-1-62832-820-2 (pbk)
ISBN 978-1-64000-418-4 (eBook)
Subjects: LCSH: Karts (Automobiles)—Juvenile literature.
Classification: LCC TL236.5.G57 2021 / DDC 629.228/5—dc23

CCSS: RI.1.1, 2, 4, 5, 6, 7; RI.2.2, 5, 6, 7, 10; RI.3.1, 5, 7, 8;
RF.1.1, 3, 4; RF.2.3, 4

First Edition HC 9 8 7 6 5 4 3 2 1
First Edition PBK 9 8 7 6 5 4 3 2 1

Table of Contents

The International Kart Federation (IKF) was formed in 1957.

Kart racing, or karting, features small vehicles. The first kart was built in 1956. It was powered by a lawnmower **engine**.

engine a machine that makes a vehicle move by burning fuel

The kart's frame sits about one inch (2.5 cm) off the ground.

Karts sit low to the ground.
They can weigh 165 to more than 300 pounds (74.8–136 kg). A well-built **chassis** (*CHA-see*) keeps the kart from rolling over. Some karts have a roll cage. This metal frame protects the driver during rollovers.

chassis the base frame of a vehicle

Kart races take place on streets, tracks, or circuits.

There are several kinds of karts and kart races. Some races take place on dirt tracks. Other races are on paved **circuits** built just for karting.

circuits closed routes that begin and end in the same place

Sprint karting takes place on road circuits. Drivers skillfully speed through sharp curves. Races last about 15 minutes. Points are awarded for a team's number of entries, finishing position, and races completed.

Sprint kart circuits are about one mile (1.6 km) long.

Enduro karts go up to 90 miles (145 km) per hour. Enduro kart races last 30 to 60 minutes. Team members take turns driving in 6 to 24 hour races.

Enduro kart drivers lie down while driving.

Many pro drivers got their start in kart racing.

In **speedway** races, drivers make only left-hand turns. The kart's chassis is built specifically for these oval tracks. It gives better **traction** as the kart moves.

speedway dirt or paved oval-shaped tracks

traction the grip of a tire on the ground

Some superkarts can compete against racing cars and motorcycles.

Superkarts almost look like race cars. They are more **aerodynamic** than other karts. They can go more than 160 miles (257 km) per hour!

aerodynamic having a shape that allows air to move smoothly over the surface

Karting is the safest racing sport. But karts do not have many safety features. Most do not have seatbelts. Instead, drivers wear helmets and protective suits.

A neck collar helps to support the driver's neck during a race.

Many local tracks allow people of all ages to try kart racing.

Professionals race in **leagues** around the world. But kids as young as five can learn how to race karts. Find a kart racing track and try this amazing sport for yourself!

leagues groups of teams or individuals that compete against each other

Driver Spotlight: Mia Chapman

Mia Chapman lives in Arizona. She is a regular teenager. But she is also a race kart driver. By 2019, Mia had won seven championships racing trophy karts. Trophy karts are small versions of off-road trophy trucks. These vehicles are used in high-speed desert races. Mia got her first trophy kart when she was just six years old! At first she was afraid of it. Now she loves racing.

Read More

Adamson, Thomas K. *Karts*. Minneapolis: Bellwether Media, 2019.

Barger, Jeff. *Go-Karts*. Vero Beach, Fla.: Rourke Educational Media, 2016.

Huddleston, Emma. *Karts*. Minnetonka, Minn.: Kaleidoscope, 2019.

Websites

Kiddle: Auto Racing Facts for Kids
https://kids.kiddle.co/Auto_racing
Learn about karts and other race cars.

KidzSearch: Kart Racing
https://wiki.kidzsearch.com/wiki/Kart_racing
Read more about kart racing.

PBS Kids: Kart Kingdom
https://pbskids.org/kartkingdom/
Use critical thinking to complete races.

Note: Every effort has been made to ensure that the websites listed above are suitable for children, that they have educational value, and that they contain no inappropriate material. However, because of the nature of the Internet, it is impossible to guarantee that these sites will remain active indefinitely or that their contents will not be altered.